JOURNEY INN

A Place of Infinite Possibility

By

Mychal Mills

ISBN 978-0-9998269-0-4

Library of Congress Control Number: 2018900724

Printed by DiggyPOD, Inc., in the United States of America.

First printing, 2018.

To my parents, Deneise and George, for all the
Love and Support on this Journey. Thank You!

To all the soul-ships, partners in healing,

partners in exploring, soul families,

soul brothers, soul sisters.

I am a reflection of you.

I love you.

*My **dedication** is this entire book.*
*This book is an expression of **Self**.*
*From my **soul** to yours.*
*From my **journey** to yours.*
*From my **eye** to yours.*
*We are **one** in the same.*
*No my, just **I**.*
Infinite, Limitless.

Peace ~ Love ~ Presence

~ Soul Flow ~

Essence

My Purpose and Existence

God

I Am ~ Am I

Beyond

Look at me,
Look at me and tell me what you see.
Look at me,
See me,
Understand me,
Understand, that you can't understand me,
Accept me,
Appreciate me,
Cherish me,
For what you see,
For what you don't see.

Look at me,
A natural spring of pure love.
Don't you see my only intention is love?
Do you see the green lantern glowing in my chest?
Do you see the light illuminating so bright?
The sun, the stars, and the moon at night,
Are all within me.
Do you see me?
Look at me.

Look at me,
See me, but don't see me.
Love me,
Love me for what you see,
Love me for what you don't see,
Love me for me.
Look at me,
Look beyond what the eyes can see,
Look beyond what the ego can see,
Then you will see,
And you will see me,
Look at me...

Vulnerable

I rather have that awkward wave,
With no wave back,
Than to not wave at all.
I am strong enough to withstand the embarrassment,
You see, I have fallen many times before,
I have, and will, get back up.
Let my wave be a symbol that my heart is open
with no shame,
How dare I put up walls because of society's frame?
A standard picture of what is normal.
But I'm here to tell you
that my love cannot be contained.
When all else is lost, my love is all that remains.
The "I" is all that remains.
I am unbounded by misery's chains,
My intention is to wave, why should I refrain in fear
that yours aren't the same?
My love does not change just because your love is
not the same,
I will wave with no expectation of a wave back,
Because I have learned that unconditional love
doesn't always love back.
Unconditional love is all that we lack.
If our love is unconditioned, then we will always
wave back.
My wave is a reflection of me,
So when I wave to you, I only see me
It's in the absence of unity
that we see the division between you and me.
From my heart and for all to see, open and honestly,
I wave, no shame, no blame,
I love, no attachment, no frame,
I will wave again, I will love again...

Pinky and the Brain (Part 1)

Hey Brain,
What do you want to do tonight?
The same thing we do every night Pinky,
Try to take over the world!
The fool in me once wanted to change the world,
But I found that I could only change
the eyes of the "I" that perceive the world.
A world not separate of me, but within me,
U-N-I-T-Why do I say we when all there is, is me?
If there's only the "I" then there is no "we".
How could I ever look down on you
without looking down on me?
If we are all one, how could there can be, a two?
There's no "me" without "you"
then how could I perceive anything separate of you?
When I see you I see me, but when you see me
do you see you? Or do you see me?
Through the eye of the I,
I can only see one Eye.
They say, watch out for the devil in disguise!
What if I told you that the devil's in the eyes?
The devil of the eye, that's the true devil in disguise.
That devil in demise turns to heaven in the eyes,
Then the God in you will rise.
The God in you, the I in you, the essential,
The All is mental, this world is mental.
For good or for bad is the mind's judgmental,
To respond or react is your own potential.
Now let me rewind to that child's mind –
When Pinky asks Brain what he wants to do tonight,
Brain will respond, I am taking over the world!
And I will start within, because I am the world...

Friday Night

Tonight will be different
Tonight, I am infant,
Tonight is dedicated to you,
Excuse me, I meant to say me,
This is not a Friday night going out,
It's a Friday night going in.

I'll spend the evening with my lover, best friend and
kin,
Tonight I will cater to me, myself, and I,
It's been eternity since the last time.

Our conversation will be the best,
One that'll put me, myself, and I to the test.
Me will begin with theories of revolution as the
only evolution,
Myself will contest the main issue is Mother Earth
so we must address environmental pollution,
And I will trump all, saying we have lost the
essence of our soul,
And the revolution
should be to return to our natural home.

Then we will tune into our vision,
Not television,
But the vision aligned with the mission,
of following our guiding light through intuition.
Dream wise, because this is the place where dreams
become fruition,
Thoughts become decision,
And actions reflect ambition.

Tonight, I will be poetry,
A dedication to love,
Quiet the mind and let inspiration rise above,
I will write about the first time I fell in love,
With myself,
Better late than never,
I was once told that patience is fully understood
when you realize you are forever.
Time is no factor because it's the journey that
brought us together.

Tonight, I'm going within,
And the words you hear are reflection of my soul.
Tonight will be different,
Tonight, I am infant,
Tonight is limitless,
Tonight is infinite...

Balloons

Release, to the sky,
Let go of balloons, string by string.
I release, out of love to let go,
I release, out of love to let flow,
I release, out of love to let grow.
Emptiness has never felt so fulfilling.

Balloons, drifting through the sky,
Filled with air, moving with air,
Releasing the weight holding it down,
The ego holding it down,
The perception holding it down.
The weight of all physical desire,
Let go of the body to move higher.

Let mind go,
Let imagination flow,
Let spirit grow,
I now know, I don't know,
Let Go, Let Flow, Let Grow...

Airplane Mode

Turn off your wi-fi,
Turn on your sci-fi,
In this moment of gravity's defy,
I am departing from Mother Earth to fly,
High, above clouds and skies,
I am now going within.

Turn off your wi-fi,
Turn on your sci-fi,
Shift focus to your mind's eye,
Follow the breath slowly,
Ready for departure,
I am now within...

....

I am home
Within, quiet hymns of air caressing nostril hairs,
A place of content and simplicity,
Taking less and gaining more.

I am home
Alone, within the all,
I can see the all,
When God spoke to me, I answered me.

I am home
Doing doing being,
Being being doing,
Doing in the being,
Being in the doing.

I am home
I wrote history in perception,
I create future with the Presence,
I give these presents,
All of my Presence.

I am home
A Yin to a Yang,
Colors constantly change,
Maybe there's no difference,
The difference is the preference.

I am home
Trees roots and leaves,
Mountains rocks and peaks,
Maybe I stand tall,
Maybe I sit small.

I am home
In stillness, watching a movie in motion,
Rewind, fast forward, replay,
I decide the genre of choice,
Or maybe I don't.

I am home
Flying with Jonathan,
The seagull that is no more,
I am a refection of him,
I am more.

I am home
The rise of civilization,
The fall of great nation,
A place of nonexistence,
The tree of knowledge, full of inquiries and
answers.

I am home
Homeless to the thing I call home,
For I know no home,
But the journey to return home,
I am home ...

Breath Insight

The ups and downs,
The smiles and frowns.
The good the bad,
The happy the sad.

The clear the cloudy,
The mountains the valleys.
The creation and destruction,
The ease the obstruction.

The tall the small,
The rise and the fall.
The peace and the chaos,
The debt the payoff.

The love the hate,
The choice the fate.
The beginning the end,
The enemy the friend.

The birth the death,
The goodwill and theft.
The success the fail,
The inhale the exhale.

Breath in Bless,
Breath out stress.
I know one, because I have felt both –
The constant change of nature's beauty,
The pendulum of the universe is always shifting...

Oneness of Life

One Moment
One Breath
One Purpose
One Journey
One Experience
One Love
One Universe
One Energy
One Path
One Ending
One Beginning
One Life

Nothingness
Emptiness
Infinitely
Eternally...

Everyday

Today is the day
where I can rejoice in all I did,
But more importantly, in all I am.
I am physical,
To nurture beings and elevate higher.
I am spiritual,
Eternally embedded in the earth, sea, air, and fire.
A creator, savior, divine maker,
In my infinite Presence,
I save the world, then come home to my essence.
An alchemist in its purest form,
Love's role continues to transform.
I love all that I did
and I love all that I am.
Mother Earth,
Father Sky,
Seek balance from inside,
Today is the day,
As it is each and every day,
To celebrate in my own unique way...

I LIVE (≠) MY BEAUTIFUL TRUTH

Fire

Injustice and Oppression

World Suffering

Breaking Free from the Program

The Other

Do you ever wonder how it feels?
To be the other, the outcast, the problem?
The type that a badge claiming self-defense from a
demon will solve.

Will you ever face the fatal dilemma
when both options are right?
My eyes on his waist,
I see the trigger happy in his face,
Should I put my hands up again or stand up to
fight?

I wish you knew this feeling of being brought up in
a society where you don't matter,
In every thought and decision you remain the latter,
Would you be able to father and raise a black
family?
That's in a continuous battle with society's calamity,
Every look in the mirror the man you see is not the
man you dreamed to be,
You became everything society has made you to be,
Bitter and black, bruised and cracked,
Reminded about everything you lack.

Now mister, I ask,
Do you ever imagine how it feels?
Because what I failed to mention is this is a pain
that never heals.
For my back still peals from the whips my ancestors
received in your fields.
You can't just walk a mile in these shoes of
discomfort,
Without putting in 400 years of mental captivity and
fieldwork.

This is nothing you can learn from the lyrics of
these so-called hip hop songs,
So before I carry on, you need to be aware that to be
oppressed is to be strong.

For too long society has told me my way of thinking
is wrong,
For the simple fact that I'm awake and thinking is
wrong,
Now I see, from the weakness in your knees and the
tremble in your voice,
This struggle is not for you –
You're lucky you have a choice...

My Dedication

This is my dedication to you,
I promise to speak my truth – my whole truth and
nothing but my truth, so help me..

Well, let's just forget that next line,
because it usually begins by lying,
We create justice for lies
but there's no justice for lives.

Our justice system commits crimes to punish
crimes,
We don't participate,
but we're first in line to criticize.
When it comes to inaction, there's no difference
between the awake and those who are blind,
True change, is when we begin to perceive beyond
our own eyes,
Extending hands for compromise.

I pledge allegiance,
Not to a flag or a nation,
Not to the one that has created a society of
dehumanization,
Disenfranchised, economic inequality, and mass
incarceration,
Miseducation, corruption, deception and CIA
assassinations,
CIA assassinations!
Police assassinations!
Political assassinations!
Religious assassinations!

Things haven't changed, like Tupac's *war on the
streets*,

There's still *war in the Middle East,*
Instead of war on poverty,
There's still *war on drugs, so the police can bother*
me.

They say the United States is like the world police,
That makes a lot of sense –
Because Libya must resemble Treyvon,
Vietnam and Freddie Gray sang the same song,
Mike Brown is a mirror of Iraq,
Both Jaquan and Afghanistan were shot in the back.
Too many countries and too many names,
We lost space in our conscience and in our graves,
And we can't forget about our own,
A society that murders its own.

Both Flint and Sandra were dealt the same fate,
It's the ideological divisions in our minds that we
create.
Whether across the world or right here in America,
It's all the same hate –
That hate that perpetuates to leave masses in an
oppressed mind state,
The slave of an inmate, they make slaves out of
inmates.

Another conflict, another shooting, another
uprising,
The oppressed have been down too long,
Now they're uprising,
The wisdom of our own,
We can find wisdom within our own,
That's the true meaning of a people up rising,
Our young Kings and Queens are up rising,
Rise to your crown, don't let anything bring you
down!

Blexcellence

Blexcellence,
Black excellence!
Magnificent,
Heaven sent,
Dragged through slavery's hell and back again,
Breaking free from the shackles,
Maya Angelou's I rise again,
We rise again!
We hear the echoes of revolutionary cries,
From Ferguson to Haiti to Palestine,
To the Dakota's pipeline –
they took another lifeline,
To Baltimore, and too many more,
We send eulogies to complacency's demise,
We rise, we rise, we rise.

Blexcellence,
Black excellence!
A dream of a dream,
Being the dream of Dr. King,
A dream's offspring,
To inspire others to dream.
A dream for freedom to sing,
For our young Kings and Queens,
To take the baton and carry on,
To the mountain tops of the promised land,
Our minds are the promised land,
To realize the essence of our potential,
We must break free from the prisons of the mental.

Blexcellence,
Black excellence!
More than 400 years of excellence,
Your excellence is more ancient and prevalent,
Religion thrives in the seeds of Kemetic,
Philosophy is alive and engrained in Hermetic,
Your astrology of the universe remains prophetic,
From Washington DC to Egypt,
your architecture is masterful and aesthetic,
These are the fruits of your hidden colors,
Don't you forget it!

Blexcellence,
Black excellence!
More than entertainment and athletics,
Your divine nature remains succulent,
Your fashion breeds elegance,
Fruitful and beautiful,
There is nothing they can do to you,
To hide the truth of you,
We pay homage to the past,
And give hope to the future,
By standing powerful in the present,
We are all you,
Black excellence,
Your greatness is genetic!

World Story

I speak to you out of love,
But this is not a love story,
This will never be the Allie and Noah *Notebook*
story,
There is no fairytale ending to this story,
This is a war story, thousands of children in the path
of drones story,
A father's collect call to his daughter from a prison
phone story,
This is a he came out, now he can't go home story,
A young woman's comfort in a man's groan story,
A young man's finding love and family in a gang
story,
An America home of the brave story,
But we have people homeless on the street,
so they can only be brave story,
Cause there is no home when inequalities and
injustices roam story,
And these next lines are for the politicians and
leaders that built promises on mountains of lies,
From Baltimore to Haiti to Palestine,
We hear the echoes of revolutionary cries,
We are witness democracy's demise,
We the oppressed, our energy can't be suppressed,
But like the words of Maya Angelou's soul,
We Rise..

If you don't nourish your body, how can you
develop your mind?
If you're lost in your mind, how can you discover
your soul?

No, this is not a love story,
This is a survival story,
Let my compassion heal and revive you story,
A single mother's overnight shift straight to a 9 to 5 story,
A father's second chance home from prison to provide story,
A peace sequel to break the racial divide story,
A we the people, through the divine created uniquely equal story,
No, this is not a love story,
This is my story, your story, our story...

Unspoken Letters

Dear Brother,
You taught me to be the best man I can be,
You taught me to be the best man I can be,
By showing me everything I didn't want to be,
Everything I didn't want to see in the cries from our
mother's eyes,
Not knowing if her son is going to make it home
alive,
In the nine to five, you chose the nine,
Steady looking up to five,
You chose blood over blood,
Do you know the difference between blood?
Not of a mother and father,
Not of your own brother,
Not of your son and daughter,
You done lost sight of who you are,
False flagging, emotions lagging,
Imagine your family picture's caption,
MIA missing in action,
The irony, to write a letter to me from the county,
When you could have walked three blocks to see
me,
Instead, you wrote in that letter how you seen me on
APTV,
But you could have walked three blocks to see me,
Believe me, I would respond if need be,
Forgiveness from others is just too easy,
It's time to see the uneasy,
Take control of the correction and look at mirror
reflection,
I can care less about the crimes they say you
commit,

Why I would I continue to inflate stereotypes of a
justice system I don't agree with?
But you couldn't see it,
Because pawns are mindless,
They use their mind less,
They abuse their own flesh,
They use till none left,
Man, there's none left,
Growing up, the bond was strong,
Those days have been gone,
I felt that void for too long,
Emotions felt, I moved on,
Another letter, same song,
But the funniest part of it all,
I became a Big Brother and mentor to feel
something I never had,
And one day your son will do the same,
When he becomes a better father than his own dad...

Explosions

Do you trust me? Okay good,
Follow these instructions,
Every step is important,
Open your hands,
Hold this grenade,
Be with this grenade,
Absorb this grenade,
Do you trust me? Okay good,
Hold it tight,
As of if your world would end if it ever slipped
from your hands,
As if tears of blood would flood the mouths of
infant children,
Hold it tightly,
Caress the rough exterior as if every blemish was a
mistaken identity,
Feel the warmth,
That warmth is from hands of the past that weren't
strong enough to hold on,
But none of that matters, cause you're here now,
Do you trust me? Okay good,
Please listen closely,
These next steps hold the fate of your destiny,
Open your hands,
Focus your eyes inside of the grenade,
Do you see it?
Look deeper,
Look deeper,
Look deeper,
Do you trust me? Okay good,
But please tell me,
Do you trust you?
Cause the final step is all about you,

Insecurity, fear, vulnerability will haunt your
nightmares,
Can you face demons in the darkest of nights?
And be saved by your own knight in shining armor,
Yourself,
This final step is no place for thinking,
They will be the detours to your happiness,
Look at the pin of the grenade,
Take a deep breath in,
Breathe out,
Pull the pin out quickly, quickly
Do not hesitate,
Do not stutter,
Do not run from the unknown,
Jump from the plank into a sea of faith,
Melt your soul into dreams of the everlasting,
No matter what, you are always everlasting,
I promise you I won't steer you wrong,
Pull the pin out of grenade right now,
Please do it now,
Do it right now!
…
I love you, and now, you can finally see it,
My love explodes like grenades,
Leaving corpses of those who can't go beyond the
surface of fairytale love,
Others have been burnt from the light,
Because it was too bright for their level of sight,
Sometimes we avoid caution tape because others
have been hurt there,
But sometimes, we have to put faith into fear to find
that love comes in all forms,
The most dangerous is also the deepest and most
warm...

Organized Crime

I'm glad they caught him,
I am glad they caught him,
Murder suspect in the first degree,
One dead to the street,
Another dead to the system,
That's what they call a two for one,
Buy one, get one free,
Dead one, chain one's feet,
Prison systems feed off crime in these streets,

Am I glad they caught him?
When he is not the problem, but the symptom of a
broken system,
But there's no diagnosis,
And they don't want you to know this,
Because then you'd notice, this pipeline looks all
too familiar,
Too many graduate school to get first degree behind
bars,
These streets didn't raise him,
The system is the one that gave him, gun in hand,
Taught by schools with no book in hand,
The type of school you wait 20 years to give them a
book,
You throw them the book – life sentence!
Wars on drugs seem double sided,
Creating the problem, then they hide it,
Arresting the drug dealer,
But not the one who supplied it,
We know who supplied it.

Am I glad they caught him?
In a system where 'no snitching' seems to be the
best defense.

Some of you forgot, Malcolm and Martin were
surrounded by informants,
And informants against the system go missing,
Too many undocumented and not talking about
immigrants,
These crimes well organized and long strategized,
To program our minds,
Masses incarcerated, male dominated,
Mothers left to raise sons in a culture that oppresses
women,
True colors have been hidden,
Self-fulfilling prophecies long written,
Replacing plantations with the prison,
Willie Lynch must have been a prophet.

Am I glad they caught him?
Somewhere lost in between the first and thirteenth,
Legalized slavery and the right to free speech,
We lost both,
Shackled to the feet and programmed in the brain,
Voiceless words and lost names,
Silenced and constrained,
Rat race, chasing the money and the fame,
Hiding emotions in sex and drugs to numb away the
pain,
The old civil rights pray upon a change,
The appearance is different,
But the matrix is the same,
He was just another pawn on the chessboard,
Lost in the game.

Am I glad they caught him?
He was caught a long, long time ago,
We just didn't know it…

The Program

I am the program,
I systematically download my instructions into your
belief..
You are a patriot of America, the land of
opportunity,
You have faith in anything I speak – let's call this
religion to make it easy,
You join our military to be all you can be,
You shed the blood of masses overseas to keep your
country "free",
You are trained to terminate on sight instead of to
see,
You are a result of blind conspiracy,
Bullets mysteriously find their way to those who go
off course to seek,
You served me well, my veteran,
Now go to the local soup kitchen to eat,
And don't forget to share your favorite war story.

I am the program,
I create your life in a playground box to keep you in
sync,
No need for you to think, just follow my
instructions, download complete..
You are a G up in these streets,
You rap nursery rhymes over my beats,
Your women twerk half naked over my beats,
You rather buy swag than food for your kids to eat,
You allow my welfare system to feed,
More than just food, I become their need,
To learn complacency and never bite the hand that
feeds,
Broken hoop dreams turned to dope fiends,

You sold your soul for the American slave dream,
You are limited by two, the bloods and crips, the
red and blue,
But the only blue is when the police come through,
and gun shots stain red on you fools,
So blind, you claim to be against the man,
But you've become a mirror reflection of the man,
Wait, we went off command, just take the welfare
from my hand,
You served me well, my G, now go to your local
soup kitchen to eat, and don't forget to throw
Tyrone a coming home party,
Rather than celebrate your niece's college degree.

I am the program,
Your life is predetermined from birth to the hearse,
My entertainment controls your total sense of
worth,
You have inherited my gift as your curse,
You are the program...

Reflections

Perceptions and Curiosity

Am I what I Think I Am

Me ~ Myself ~ I

Inner Voice

Who?
Who told you that you aren't good enough?
Who said that you aren't smart, that your mind is
mediocre?
Who showed you that your life won't be what you
dreamed it to be?
Who told you everything's hard, there's ups and
downs, you just need to deal with it?
Who said you were black and ugly?
That skin color matters?
Who said you are white privilege, that status is
necessary and others need to suffer to get ahead?
Who told you that you need to fit in, look to par and
comply with society's norms?
Who told you that you are worthless?
Who taught you to go through the motions, get
through the day, dwell on the pain of the past, and
stress over the future? Who??
Who said that you need to change to be accepted?
Who taught you this substandard mind state that
you carry with you right now?
Who gave you this misery that eats away at you
every single day and drives you to the suicide of
complacency?
Who told you that you are not perfect?
Who told you not to be you?

It was me, that's who,
No, not the person in front of you now,
But the person that sits in your mind,
Because there's nothing I can feed you that you
don't accept,

And there's nothing I can tell you that you didn't
already believe,
We say this misery is from everything else, when,
in actuality, it circles back to self,
These self-inflicted wounds are the eve of
destruction,
The seeds of reproduction, the endless cycle of
suffering,
It was I – when we replace I and you,
Then we find all paths lead back to you,
I is the beginning and end, your best or worst
friend,
Do you love yourself as whole or do you love your
flaws?
We make mistakes and claim nobody can be perfect
to justify the cause,
All of our *I am's* and *I am nots* stem back to our
thoughts,
We are storytellers of our own truth and we are the
main character,
We are artists that paint perception of our reality,
In reality, we travel further and further from pure
essence and absolute truth,
Because we have yet to release all the labels society
has put on you,
Who are you?
Who am I?
I am not what you see,
What you see is what you see,
Maybe it's best for us not to see,
Maybe it's best to just feel and to be...

Grateful Encounters (4)

To the joyless receiving clerk,
And many, many other Trump supporters that
believe we need to stop immigration,
Well I'm ashamed to say I completely agree,
You see, we don't need any more people in this
country because we have yet to care for our own,
We cannot let others in if we haven't mastered the
program in our home,
These others come with expectation of freedom and
equality,
It takes too long to break their mindstate and mold
them into American society,
How dare they come here for free and gain on this
land tax free,
And then ask for citizenship relief?
What a tragedy, for people to live without Uncle
Sam reaching in their pockets,
Isn't that one of the reasons we fought for
independence?
These others have been a burden on our economic
and healthcare system,
Too many to round up and arrest them,
We need to build a great giant wall, about a hundred
feet tall,
Yes, that should keep them out,
Without a doubt we will become that strong,
powerful nation once again,
And we can continue with the oh so popular *God
Bless America* and no one else because we are one
nation, under God, indivisible, with liberty and
justice for all,
Expect for the "all" that have been breaking our
immigration laws,

We'll just have to "Indian give" those blessings,
And redistribute them in an equitable way from the
top down,
From the top down, you will get your crumbs if you
follow suit and don't act loud,
But if you act proud, some CIA special operations
will have to come through and crack down,
And we know how the CIA has come to our
communities to bring crack down,
Well, if I had to agree to stop immigration,
It would be for very different reasons,
I don't want any more people to come to this
country with the false ideology that this is the land
of opportunity,
Well actually it is – to lose your sense of culture, of
family, of community, of self,
And become Americanized,
This country has a great education system in
teaching your children hate, greed, superficial status
And what schools feed for lunch is the best, of the
worst,
The music and entertainment will program you into
believing you are one of them,
Matter of fact, why don't you bleach your skin and
dye your hair so you look like you're one of them,
And begin acting like you're one of them –
download complete – you are now on repeat,
This country will eat away at your vulnerability and
steal your innocence,
And replace it with the deepest obsessions and
coldest of bitterness,
So you are much, much better off staying where you
are,
Because there is nothing wrong with being poor in
possession and rich in spirit,

There is nothing wrong with living among nature when this country fears it,
There is nothing wrong with having blind eyes, for no man made division can divide I,
We are all one, from the earth to the sun,
We are all connected..
So please, please remember – the grass isn't always greener,
Especially when it's genetically modified...

Grateful Encounters (2)

To the woman who told me there's no time to get calm,
Well I guess your time is better spent in chaos,
Life's cost, of choosing stress over blessed,
The wrinkles on your face show the storyline you chose to tell the world,
Can you imagine your life choices were rolled over to the next?
Karma, the misery of today becomes tomorrow,
And life decisions are followed by sorrow,
Happiness borrowed, just to return to the pain of tomorrow,
How will you live today knowing it will affect your tomorrow?

Background Bliss

Have you ever paused to listen to the background?
We are so caught up in the doing that we are
mindless of what we're doing,
And neglect that there's a background,
The background sounds of nature's intercourse,
The background pulse of your heart' rate,
For faster or slower your life's fate,
The background 80's music in department stores,
The background static from the radio we try our
best to ignore,
The background crashing of ocean waves along the
shore,
The background of birds chirping as the sun rises,
daily reminders of our heart's rising,
The background conversation, words and
interaction,
The background sigh of a cry for help,
The background of the breath as air funnels through
the nostril to the stomach,
And the background voices in the mind, running
and running,
Background carries beauty, truth, chaos, elegance,
suffering, the entire storyline of your world,
Background is always on repeat,
When we silence our minds to hear the background,
We may realize there is no background,
The background is the all but our mind's
unconscious chatter overpowers it all..

The Greatest Love Story

I invite you in,
I invite you into my thoughts,
Stay there, because thoughts are sometimes better
than reality,
I won't lose there, I won't lose you there,
You are safe there,
The choice between a great love and a great story,
The difference between fiction and non-fiction,
Fairytales and tombstones,
Realty is full of tombstones,
A tombstone for death,
A tombstone when you left,
A tombstone for a last breath,
A tombstone for expectation and sadness,
The blossom of a flower will always die,
In reality, I will remember the one that set the
standard,
The one that moved mountains of doubt and
dissipated scars,
Like birds released from a cage she set all fears
free,
All this just to become the death of me,
Why give me life if your plans aren't to save it?
But in my thoughts, it's different,
You're always there, always sincere,
You disappear and reappear,
You are the peace to my tear,
Love is better told as a story than lived,
I can rearrange the end to the point of no end,
In the greatest love I'll ever know,
My thoughts of you are better than the reality of
you,
Reality will perish in the earth,

And leave you in the dark wondering what was this worth,
What was this curse, that left my emotions battered and bruised,
Lost and confused in reality of lies,
Echoes from your last words buried in the loneliest night's cries,
But a story, a story can be told over and over,
Revised and amended as it gets older so each ending is a new beginning,
And I'm never left guessing like God manipulating his own blessing,
I know you're still with me, I know you're still here,
So would I choose a great love or a great story?
A great story or a great love?
Is there a difference?
I am deceived from the thoughts of me and perceive the reality of you,
Is there a difference?
Between love's reality and the story I think in my mind's eye,
Is there a difference?
In reality, I create my own reality from my thoughts of reality,
I can love the thoughts that become the reality of you,
Is there a difference?
Or maybe this is just an unending story,
An undying love,
A love as a story, A story of love,
You are my greatest imagination and best reality,
My thoughts wouldn't exist without the reality of you,
The only love story is you...

Wonder World

I think and I think then I think that I think so I think
and I think and I think,
Therefore I Am,
I think then thought is reflection of I Am,
The more I think the more I Am,
Thousands of thoughts thousands I Am's,
How can one man be so many I Am's?

I think that I Am then I think that I'm not,
So I continue to think, why not?
Why do I think that I Am and why do I think that
I'm not?
Who's in control of all these conflicting thoughts?
Who's the author of this plot?
I think that I Am and I think that I'm not.

I think that I Am but am I what I think?
I was taught to think before I could think,
So when I think, is it my think?
Or is it the think from the one that taught me to
think?
They say two of the most powerful words are I Am,
But if I think that I Am from the one that taught me
to think,
Am I what I think I Am or am I the Am from the
one who taught me I Am?
Maybe I Am..

I think and I think then I think that I think so I think
and I think and I think,
Therefore I Am,
The masculine energizes the I and the feminine
births the Am,

When masculine and feminine are in balance so is
the I Am,
For the one who lacks masculinity their Am is
created from the I of another,
The I of another with no control of Am,
So when you think again, ask yourself who's in
control of I Am,
I think that I Am,
Remove the think,
I Am...

Zombie

Sleep
Wake up
Shower
Brush teeth
Get dressed
Job
Work as instructed
Work
Work has concluded
Home
Dinner
TV
Sleep
Tomorrow – Repeat

Sleep
Wake up
Shower
Brush teeth
Get dressed
Job
Work as instructed
Work
Work has concluded
Home
Dinner
TV
Sleep
Tomorrow – Repeat

You are sleep
Life on repeat
Follow steps 1 through 14
Your mind on auto pilot
Your body in daily routine

Sleep
Wake up
Shower
Brush teeth
Get dressed
Job
Work as instructed
Work
Work has concluded
Home
Dinner
TV
Sleep
Tomorrow – Repeat

Gym Diaries

It's been a long, long day,
And it's time for that quick fix,
It's usually a drink, then binge on Netflix,
But today, neither of those will do the trick,
In need of something stronger,
I've been weak in my knees,
Weak in my voice,
Maybe I'll go to the gym so I can at least look a
little stronger,
Let's double up on the weight like all the emotion I
swallowed today,
25 pounds for hiding inside instead of speaking my
mind,
Another 25 for choosing ego over pride,
Another 25 for reacting another time the mirror
image to my demise,
Forget it, let's just max out,
Because lately I've been feeling emotionally maxed
out,
I look into the mirror for a quick flex,
You see, the mirror and I have a love hate
relationship,
At times it drags my self-esteem through the valleys
of death,
And other times it convinces me hope will see
another day,
To love myself in its own unique way,
What will it show me today?
Side eye, I look at the competition,
They're in my mirror flexing,
I can't help but notice my bicep is bigger than your
calf,
The ego looks at half,

And compares what you lack,
I see your fault when only focused on part,
Instead of whole,
Each one of us is whole
And play a collective role,
In consciousness,
But I have been stuck in this unconsciousness,
Emotion and self-esteem,
I am the victim and offender in my own horror
dream,
In this planet of fitness,
They say no judgement and no critics,
But I am the worst of my own,
I give and receive based on the beliefs I was taught
to perceive,
A mind not free will never conceive the highest it
can achieve,
Building strength to this physical,
And neglecting to train the mental,
If the mind is the all,
I spent too much time in a gym,
Not training at all...

Holiday Spirit

Nope, sorry I don't celebrate this holiday,
No, not that holiday either,
Well let me explain –
Every day is Valentine's day,
A reason to fall in love all over again,
With the beauty life has to offer,
Should I buy chocolate to prove it?
Every day is a day of independence,
Where I can be an infinite free mind,
Souls can never be captive like weak minds,
This country has the highest incarcerated population
in the world, think about it,
Every day is my birthday,
Each day I am born again in a constant state of
renewal,
My days are like blank canvases and I'm the
paintbrush,
Every day is the so-called Christmas,
A reason to give presents by focusing on the
presence,
This is the gift from the inside that can't be seen,
And it certainly doesn't come down a chimney,
That leads me to this memorial day,
Well, today and everyday are memorial if I live in
the now,
I won't need to recognize the past,
Because I celebrate the present moment and
everyone in it,
Of course, I am always thankful and giving,
Why do I need to slaughter a turkey to prove that?
That's kind of an oxymoron, right?
And labor, is that something to celebrate?
I'm actually trying to work less and live more,

We are the most overworked nation in the world,
But what are we working for?
Oh yes, I do have a dream,
I don't think that dream was for a day off and
dedicated boulevards turned into war zones,
It's kind of funny the name MLK is on everything,
But the spirit of his teachings died with him,
By the way, the people who killed him are still
around,
Oh, my favorite, the discovery of America,
Well, let's just ask the redskins what they think
about it,
They'll probably say only a few people are upset
about it,
They're right, there would probably be more if the
natives weren't slaughtered to extinction,
And huddled into 2% of their stolen land just to be
pipelined over,
I bet you they wish they thought of that wall idea a
long time ago,
Of course, any immigration questions should be
referred to them,
Oh, and that last one, I don't acknowledge,
I took my mask off a long time ago,
I can only be me, why focus on fantasy?

Parable of Life

When he lost mobility in his legs,
He wished to walk,
When he was blinded from the eyes,
He wished to see,
When sound became deaf to his ears,
He wished to hear,
When his tongue became numb to flavor,
He wished to taste,
When he no longer recognized scent,
He wished to smell,
When he lost the ability to touch,
He wished to feel,
When he reached the end of his life,
He wished to live,
As spirit, he looked back on his life,
And saw a man who wished for the things he didn't have,
Instead of appreciating the abundance in his grasp,
He was too focused on endings that he missed all new beginnings,
Each and every day we are born again,
It's up to us how to perceive it...

Miles Apart

Distant man, from a distant land,
Distant culture, a distant tan,
Different hair, a different strand,
Distant music, a distant band,
Distant food, a distant brand,
Distant laws, a different ban,
Distant mind, a different plan,
I close all distance, with open hands...

Swept Under the Rug

How dare you?
No, how dare you?
You revealed your true nature without uttering one
single word,
Absurd, I know nothing about you but only your
missing integrity,
It usually takes years to unravel these character
flaws,
Normally it takes justices of law to convict this
felony,
Relationships beginning and ending at ground zero,
Ruining all chances of a warm first encounter,
Going from embracing to avoiding,
Not wanting to meet before we could meet,
Suddenly, all possibilities were left with no
possibility,
Trust me, I know what this would become, so I just
don't want it come,
Is it impossible to do the right thing when no one is
looking?
Sorry to inform you but someone is always looking,
Will you sleep tonight?
Will you regret what you did?
Will dreams haunt your conscience?
Will you ask forgiveness of yourself?
Do you even care?
Because I do,
You'll never be persecuted like the millions who've
taken this path,
But karma is waiting just around the corner,
With a hammer in one hand and open heart in the
other,

I don't know you, and maybe I've taken this too far,
But I'd rather not walk the same ground as you,
Because I've seen how you treated it,
And maybe you'd treat me the same,
Letting garbage fall from your hand without any
remorse or intention to pick it up,
It's a shame I'll only know you as the person who
swept garbage across the rug,
Maybe you've done the same in a previous
relationship,
Maybe you've swept battle cries of heartbreak to the
other side,
Maybe you've used and used and used until the
abused had nothing left,
And maybe, maybe you never even cared to look
back...

Deceptive Stereotypes

Driving along the Jersey Shore has become a lot
like dodging land mines,
Always remember these land mines,
Because the last time you drove through,
That trapline was waiting just for you,
Sirens casting lightning flashes of red and blue,
All attention on the rear view,
The clear view, I'm looking at him,
His hand on the holster he's looking at you,
As he approaches the window,
License and registration,
Is there a problem, officer?
"I said license and registration!"
Any sudden moves can put you on the evening
news,
You reach you lose,
You know these rules,
Keep your hands on the steering wheel and pray this
is not the end of your timeline,
These land mines parked along the corner of Corlies
& Norwood,
I became accustomed to take a second look,
Mind is conditioned to take that second look,
Rearview holds the fate of that second look,
But I'm ashamed to say,
I couldn't look away,
When I saw two black men walking in that same
Allenhurst neighborhood,
I had to look twice,
Just like a stereotype I looked twice,
Maybe it's not the badge but the mind that creates
these stereotypical thoughts,
That whatever black is at fault,

Whatever black is guilty until proven innocent,
But only if you're lucky enough to make it to the
precinct,
Too many bodies never make it to the precinct,
To be black comes with condition,
Second class citizen,
Oppressed to the point where you can't stand the
skin you're living in,
I guess I'm the product of the same conditioning,
That has taken too many black lives
that don't matter,
Black on black murder and white on black murder,
But we only protest the latter,
And keeps us in the same containers of thought,
To believe that they don't belong here,
That I don't belong here,
So why are they walking around here?
So why am I driving around here?
....
Preconceived judgments take second looks
....
But it's exactly those second looks that killed
Treyvon, killed Mike Brown, choked Eric Garner,
murdered Oscar Grant, Sean Bell, John Crawford,
Tamar Rice and too many others all the way back to
the open caskets of Emmitt Till,
Our minds are conditioned still,
It's not the badge that kills,
But our thoughts filled,
With fear of the inferior,
So we oppress to remain superior,
When will we stop thinking with our minds,
and return to the nature of our hearts?

Does a polar bear look a black bear differently
because of its color?
Or maybe it understands fur changes to adapt to the
weather,
But when will we learn to adapt to one another?
To bring peace to each other,
To embrace each other,
To spread love to one another...

If you live to be a
hundred, I want to
live to be a hundred
minus o n e
d a y so I
would never have to
live without you.

~ Winnie the Pooh

Intimacy

Passion and Desire

Energy and Connection

Soul Love

Soul-Mate

To my soulmate, wherever you may be,
Let me begin with describing my feelings for your
essence, your soul,
I love you deeper than any achievement or college
degree that you hold,
Deeper than what the skin, the flesh, the bones
behold,
Your energy is my sincerity,
Our sexual orientation does not sway our parity,
Clarity, we understand our connection is beyond
what eyes can see,
What I can see is beyond what these eyes can see,
Our two eyes can see a love deeper than our hands
can reach.

Universal, this movie seems to rewind,
But fast forward in time,
We have connected once again in this lifetime,
Caution, neither run away nor attach,
From this feeling, the love of a soulmate is
unmatched,
Let your light be your guidance don't steer off in
defiance,
Don't think, quiet your mind and just feel,
This script was written long before each of us was
born,
Your heart has been torn, but your inner light has
the power to heal.

Above and beyond, our love is described in that
Common song,
You are the light that shines, and I will be right by
your side,

Closer than any distance divide,
I am with you even when I'm not with you,
Our relationship doesn't depend on the physical –
We are beyond I miss you's,
We appreciate the present moment, and let go of the
past,
No need to move too fast,
We only have today,
And tomorrow is a clear forecast.

So, when the time is right,
Let our light radiate, educate, meditate,
As our souls intertwine and penetrate,
Enjoy the twists and turns, ups and downs of lover's
fate,
Carve it on a tree –
This is my testimony when I connect with my
soulmate...

This is Me

He only knows himself in times of internal conflict,
The chaotic battle has his tempered mind split,
The weather, too humid for any to enter,
But, with feelings of cold and shiver,
This is the purest winter.

It was the time from the last text that opened the
gates for regret,
How can too much too soon have led to neglect?
An abandoned heart can trigger stranger feelings,
A stranger's feeling, of being unknown to the one
you let in,
The coldest bitter minds the heart as solitude sets
in,
Forgive me,
For my imperfections have perfect intentions,
All because of my selfish selfless led to absent
mentions.

There should be a hazardous warning for this fate,
A heart in solitary confinement and emotions in
caution tape,
His mind is secluded, a path of destruction
preluded,
Cross-contaminated with resentful thoughts of a
future polluted,
I waved good-bye to the possibility of forever as
our affection diluted,
And finally, this chapter of distress has concluded...

One Night

A night to remember,
Filled with sweet laughter and drinks of joy,
It was your sincerity that turned me back to a boy,
Your smile was the warmth of sunshine,
As snow flurries sprinkled the sky.

You spoke words of wisdom far too early for your
time on earth,
Your aura set a new standard of a woman's worth,
A lady and a Queen composed of elegance and
serene,
Your beauty enhanced more fully with every
ingredient of thought you conveyed,
But what's to come out of two hearts destined
astray...

Cardiac Rehab

I just want you to know –
I didn't regret this,
And I would do it all over again,
Embracing every mistake as purpose,
Nothing is ever wasted,
Emotions have been used and abused,
Just to be used all over again,
We will be here once again,
Love will eventually recycle,
Reborn again.

Consider the death of our relationship as a rest stop
of eternity,
Your beauty will find new eyes,
Sorrow will dwindle in its own demise,
The moon will vanish, and the sun will rise,
Just to remind you that love needs both light as well
as the night,
New beginnings will plant new life,
Spring will warm the bitter frost of winter,
Vulnerabilities open like a new-born's exposure,
Animals revealed from hibernation,
Birds returning from migration.

Like Baptism's revival,
Heartbreak's sins will wash away,
Cupid's wounds will fade away,
And you will come home to that familiar place,
Where intimacy and passion spark love back into
existence,
The persistence of nature's everlasting change in
seasons,

Nothing lasts forever,
Nothing of the past will matter,
I won't matter.

And one day you may ask yourself –
Why did I care so much?
Why did I love so deeply?
Why did I allow this experience to scar my soul?
Waves of insight and question,
Begin at love's resurrection,
Looking at past relationships as prerequisites,
To find yourself,
To trust yourself,
To hug yourself,
To love yourself,
And hopefully you will see,
You were more in love with the moment, than me,
A regretful memory,
Buried like ship wrecks at the bottom of the sea,
We had to go through this storm,
To get to where we were destined to be,
Appreciating every chapter of love's journey...

Be Careful Who You Ask

She was born in demise,
She spent her life in the shadow of lies,
No father around to console her lonely cries,
Mother was the backbone, she worked double
shifts,
Double shifts became triple shifts,
Meanwhile, daughter ran the streets getting lit,
By fourteen, she was drinking and smoking, mouth
too slick,
She ran game on grown men, grew up too quick,
No guidance at home, she was forced to roam the
streets,
To learn love all on her own,
Seeking any emotional attention, sex became her
only source of affection,
Absorbing the pleasure and pain of temporary
connection,
Love ended after each erection,
She was constantly left alone to look in the mirror,
Tears drowned in her own reflection,
That's when she found her way to me and asked the
question – do you think I'm beautiful?
I paused, to ensure I answer that question right,
The next set of words could change the course of
her life,
Decisions, decisions,
Do I stay true to my belief?
Or feed her addiction?
Do I tell her the fatal truth?
Or refill her prescription?
No answer would be correct in either perception,
So I answered her question, with a suggestion,
"My Dear Beloved

Close your eyes, look into the mirror, and ask, do I think I'm beautiful?"
And this is not a yes or no question,
So please continue to question –
"Do I treat myself beautiful?"
"Do I see myself beautiful?"
"Do I carry myself beautiful?"
"Do I accept my beautiful?"
"Do I love my beautiful?"
"Do I call myself beautiful?"
Again, these are not yes or no questions,
So continue to question until you realize there is no question,
"My Dear Beloved,
Close your eyes to look into the mirror and say, I am Beautiful!
No matter how many answer that question for me, it doesn't change how I feel for me,
My worth is within me,
My love is within me,
My beauty is within me, and no one, no one!
Can take that away from me"...

Pinky and the Brain (2)

Hey Brain,
What do you want to do tonight?
The same thing we do every night Pinky,
Wait! wait! wait!
This is not going to be the same as every night,
Pinky,
Please have a seat, we need to talk,
We've been trying to do this taking over the world
thing for too long,
For way too long, I've been unconsciously going
along,
But now I'm strong, enough to say I think we need
to go our separate paths,
We've had some really good times, but they never
seem to last,
It's important not to take this personal, you always
take things so personal,
It's not you, it's me, and I've tried to tell you in our
last conversation,
Anything I say is a reflection of me,
I only reflect on what I see,
I'm saying no to you to say yes to me,
I've entered into a new state of being where I need
to just be,
Without you, free to explore what life has in store,
All the things I long for,
Lastly, please brace yourself for this,
You know how emotional you can get,
That emotion you forget,
Until it's 0 to 100, then apologies and regret.

Pinky, there's someone else,
When I'm with her, I feel what I've never felt,
I am thoughtless from her abundance of bliss and
heartfulness,
Matter fact, her name is Heart,
And she has been the pH to my chemistry from the
start,
I don't know how I've lived without her,
She balances the seas and the skies,
I listen to her, she is Marvin Gaye's rhythm and
rhyme,
And for the first time, I've been able to quiet my
mind,
To hear the whispers of the universe,
To feel sensation come and go,
No attachment, release with the flow,
Become one with the air,
The rise and the fall of my breath,
She was always there,
It was me who was lost in misery's depth,
I'm breaking free from the shackles of Samsara,
Feeling love shining in my body,
And radiating out through my aura.

So, Pinky, to answer your question about what
we're doing tonight,
Well I've already taken over the world,
And through my new found heartfulness,
I've balanced my world...

Café Bliss

I look at you,
You look at me,
I see you,
You see me.

I smile – moonlight,
You smile – sunlight,
Perfect symmetry,
Passionate chemistry.

Swarms of butterflies inside,
I try to hide,
I look down,
You turn away,
I glance back,
You circle back.

I see the serenity in your eyes,
You pierce into my soul,
I'm intrigued,
You're curious,
I smile again,
You smile more,
Best conversation, no words,
I'm a lightning strike of nerves.

Wondering what if's,
Should I break the silence?
Names aren't important,
Words can ruin the moment,
I can imagine a future with you,
That began in this café,
This moment lasts forever,
Eternity in her smile.

I'm lost in time,
But the café owner isn't,
It's coming to a close,
And I'm ready to let go,
Beauty needs freedom to grow,
Instead of holding on,
I'll allow this experience to just be,
Until the next time,
Cafe Bliss is best to reminisce...

Liar Liar

You lied, You lied!
He asked you from the valleys of depression,
And the mountain tops of insanity,
Is there someone else?
And you answered, wearing your mask of guilt,
No one else..

You said no when the truth was far from opposite,
The infidelity in finding true love outside the person
you vowed to love,
The truth more dangerous to herself than to
anybody else,
Her lie, a reflection of childhood broken promises
she made with herself,
A forgotten love, more diamond on the finger than
anything her spirit has ever felt,
My sweet soul, you have lost trust in yourself..

You should have said yes,
And that other person was revival for her flatline,
Was the hook to her punchline,
Was the person to reawaken her passion with every
drop of compassion,
Was the person that answered every cry from her
heart,
Mended every piece torn apart,
Was the finish line to her start,
Was the beauty to every mark,
Was the light to her dark,
The paintbrush to her art,
Was the ignite to her spark,
This other person was her balance,

Her harmony, the missing link to her soul,
For the first time in her life she felt complete, she
was whole.
For the next time he feels the insecurity to ask if
there's someone else,
Stand up strong with your blanket of comfort over
your heart and say yes,
And that other person is myself!
That other person was what she never knew she
wanted and everything she ever needed,
It was her journey to find abundance within herself
when all else was depleted...

Lover's Paradise

I'm going to write every ounce of my soul on the
scribbles of this paper,
Creating intimate symbols of love,
Poetry, the sacred geometry to the heart,
Then tie it to a kite,
To fly through the paradox of galaxies,
Entering twilight zones of mysteries,
Hoping it will find its way to you.

My Love
I sometimes struggle between choice and chance,
By chance, that I find my way to you,
Then make a choice that'll leave behind a trail of
tears of guilt,
Unleashing the caged regret of all the fears I built,
I'd rather choose my chance,
Then through hypnotic trance,
I can hypnotize your mind,
So you'll forever choose my stance,
Ensuring you'll never leave my side.

My Love
There will be times when your mind wonders to
distant lands of doubt,
I have been to those lands,
It is hopeless, and soulless,
Now is the time to return to your fullness,
Ego will plague you with suspicion and blurred
vision,
But this is the promise land for all you've been
wishing,
Stars aligned in our hearts,
I am here, you are here,
Let us release misplaced fear,

And walk hand in hand into sunsets,
Knowing the light begins and ends, only with you.

My Love
The core is below the surface,
Let's leave this superficial place of existence,
Beyond the despair of expectation and sadness,
Diving deeper and deeper, rising higher and higher,
I'll write our love throughout the clouds,
So when life gets rough, you can let it all fall down,
And I'll be dancing in your rain to the tune your
smile,
To remind you that the sun is always shining,
Even when you can't see it,
Always, believe it.

My Love
Do not regret this, do not look past this,
Do not mask this,
This is what love feels like connected,
Let go of what you think you know,
Unravel insecurities of past conditioning,
Open yourself to the world of uncertainty,
When curiosity befriends your inner desire,
Let us explore the depths of foundation,
Sensation, racing through our duality of serpents,
This encounter is on purpose,
Discovering fountains of dreams come true,
That dream was you.

My Love
I can't heal your Past,
And I don't know the Future,
All I know is Now is Forever,
So right Now,
Let's Stay Together...

The Invitation

As we lay on the intricate sands of the beach,
We listen to the ever-flowing ocean waves
caressing the shore,
The moon glistening along the skin of the water and
the bare of our feet,
We are engulfed in the stillness of nature at its core,
I look into the window of your soul, and ask you
what's up?
But do not get caught up in the simplicity of these
two words,
More complex than the egos that have caused world
wars,
More complex than the mind that created $E=mc^2$,
I want to know how billions of neurons ignite to
create masterpiece,
Thought and imagination,
Truth and contemplation,
Theory and revelation,
I want to know more,
Let me rephrase the question to what's in?
Tell me what's inside the soul of the universe,

I want to know everything,
I want to know all your fears,
From the daily reminders of climbing out your shell
to yell to the world, this is me and I am here!
No limitations from gender or skin tone,
A Queen cannot be lowered to ignorance from her
throne,
She dodges all of society's stones,
She is Neo in the Matrix answering the phone,
Are you ready?
I want to know your deepest temptation,

Your longing for physical, mental, and spiritual
stimulation,
I want to know how to gently caress your spine
from T1 to T5,
To bring your heart's center to life,
The vibration of my nerves ending,
Fingers curving, touching your inner desire,
To elevate and take consciousness higher,
Our minds amaze, by minds of maze,
Not locked in cage, but cleansed with sage,
Rising above this physical, we connect on the
celestial,
Exploring the space of this infinite potential,
Illuminated, shining bright from halo to this temple,
I want to sing, I want to sing sweet harmonies of
eternity,
To the hook of that Snoop Dog song,
No, not that song!
I'm glad you understand my humor may go off
course,
And of course, my voice may come off hoarse,
But quiet the mind to feel the depth of the source,

There will be, ups and downs, smile's and frowns,
Share with me, fairytales and make believes,

Make believe, make perceive, made beliefs,
Let our minds intertwine to cure disease,
Diagnosis – lack of self and overdose on identity,
The ego's enemy, to look at mirror reflection,
True love's perfection, a soul connection,
I want to know how a Queen rose to her divine state
through thousands of wars,
She strives with force,
She conquers all battles Within,

A Queen rooted in the earth, and ascended to her crown,
She wears her confidence proud, and cures despair with smile,
I want to know everything,
Show me your inner most being,
Don't just tell me what's up,
Queen, show me what's in...

Journey

Explore and Experience

Crossroads and Emotions

Past to Present

Balance of Life

I am you and you are me,
We are one,
We are energy,
In the darkness...
I have lost hope and given up too many times,
I have circled the world searching an endless mind,
I was stubborn I chose death before life,
I've screamed at the edge of a cliff with the blade of
a knife,
I was isolation in my four walls of solitary
confinement,
I was regret wondering where all the time went,
Time spent preparing for the worst because I turned
my head to the best,
I was hopeless I hoped less for a tomorrow,
I was nightmares, the night's scare, as evil praises
the night's air,
I have been a turmoil of indecision, second guessing
all intuition,
Thoughts of going missing from false realities and
mortalities,
I was alone, wishing to never come home,
I was wrong many times and held grudges with
myself,
I've forgotten the feeling of love and couldn't bear
how it felt.

I was and I have been, is the journey of my
evolution...

In the light...
I am grounded and rooted as the earth's seed,
I feel my creative expression reach its highest peak,

I do confidently to fulfill purpose and succeed not
to feed past my need but be as my world needs,
I love you as me, not always perfectly but with
perfect intention,
Perfect in mention, my compassion is mirror to my
heart's reflection,
I speak my truth from my own guidance with
understanding that it sometimes means silence,
I see from the eyes of the eye from the grounds to
the skies,
I understand peace and unity,
And I have accepted the most high,
Within me, to balance the low and the high,
And the divisions I see are only within the mind..
The journey of life,
I embrace all my darkness and light,
I am you and you are me,
Together we are balance,
We are harmony...

Disability

In my life, I have found appreciation in myself,
After seeing those with disability,
But it's been far too easy to love what others have lost,
Sight, hearing, walking, talking, eating, being able to move freely,
But if you heard it from them, you might hear a different story,
A story of struggle, grief, and pain until there's an epiphany of what was actually gained,
Freedom of mind, no longer concerned of what was lost but a realization in the value of thought,
Powerful, limitless, no longer limited by the creeds of immobility,
Our thoughts travel the earth, through the universe and back,
If there's power in thought then what do we lack?
Disability, not of the body, but of the mind,
Handicap parking spots should be for those who don't use their own mind,
I appreciate this mind, not for science, math, logic or reason,
But because I now know that this is the seed behind every emotion and feeling,
Call me Dr. Mills, because I experienced the cure for my disability,
For too long, mind has been crippled by its own thoughts,
The relentless focus on faults, I will no longer compare what has been lost,
But appreciate what I've gained..
The Mind to properly nourish body,
The Mind to create masterpieces of imagination,

The Mind to remain determined on the journey to
fulfill life purpose,
The Mind to understand it does not control love,
and love does not control you,
The Mind to express and embody truth in
everything I say and do,
The Mind to be quiet at times, when it needs to
reorganize and strategize,
The Mind to contribute to the collective
consciousness far greater than self,
To understand happiness is the best wealth,
Laughter the greatest health,
And the beauty in life is only to be felt...

Picture Pain

Sometimes I explore this feeling of pain,
Emotional pain, the type that leaves scars for
lifetimes,
And creates deep rooted fears to never walk that
path of destruction again.

That feeling when you're at the door of your love
and you hear the groan of another man,
That tone of another man,
Replaying over and over like a nightmare's
Symphony,
I never knew that sound could be so unforgiving,
And your heart sinks to your stomach, along with
broken promises of forever,
She said it would be forever,
We would always be together, through the storm
and turbulent weather,
I wonder if she told him the same fairytale,
A tear falls.

That feeling when you get a hospital call saying
your kin's strong will has been fighting along,
But divine will overpowered it all,
I melted in that call,
Body numb with every instinct to run,
Knees buckle to the weakness of denial,
How dare you ask me to identify the body when I
can barely recognize my own?
A tear falls.

Emotional pain where you want to escape reality to
a place where tears don't exist,
Where fears won't persist,

And we never chase a last kiss,
I've run courses around this experiment with pain,
Dying each time in the absorption of the inevitable,
I try to remain flexible,
But I fall victim to the susceptible truth.

Can you hear me struggle to breathe?
Can you see me grasping for the last breath because
I can't bear the pain of the new one?
These are all the painful stories, stripes and glories,
That you tell yourself I've walked through the
trenches of despair and I'm still here,
Still standing, still strong,
Still fighting, holding on,
Or maybe I'm not,
Maybe I'm not.

There's another part of the story that was forgotten,
She constantly told me that I'm emotionless, and she
was right,
He always said I didn't care what happened to him,
and he was right,
Have I learned that pain is temporary and all
feelings will pass,
Or have I become numb to the emotion?
Because the truth is, I'm more likely to cry from a
sad movie scene than any real-life crisis,
Truth is, I care about not caring,
Sometimes I struggle to show emotion to comfort
another's emotion,
Maybe I don't know how to feel,
Maybe I don't know if I feel,
Maybe I can't feel what is real,
Maybe the feeling isn't real...

Motherhood

A mother's seed is the nourishment of her being,
You are the nourishment of her being,
I am the nourishment of her being,
The drive, the desire, to fulfill and move family
higher,
Mother is the backbone,
The heartbeat and the nerves that travel from head
to toe,
She is rooted in everything I know,
My mother was more than basic needs,
She was the seed before every creed and the after to
every fracture,
Set in rapture, she is Kodak to every moment
captured.
She gave, she provided,
She thought, she decided,
She fought, she collided,
She rose, she flew,
She answered, she grew,
She clapped, she frowned,
She hugged, she smiled...

She is more than a woman,

More than a mother,

She is more...

YOLO

His body boiling with adrenaline,
His heart pumping into numbness,
Nerves running marathons through the spine with
excitement and fear,
He's finally here, his purpose once fogged with
cycles of distress is finally clear,
Feet stood at the edge of the cliff between destiny
and complacency,
He looks over the cliff into the wilderness of
uncertainty,
And behind him is the safety of his own shadow,
The internal battle,
Knowing nothing will ever be the same from this
point forward,
Not knowing anything from this point forward.

Head held high, he stood firm ready for war,
Ready for more, he's been here before,
He reminisces on past decisions,
The clashes and revisions,
The last time he was called to this place,
He knew nothing of the journey he faced,
So he rolled the dice of fate,
Praying to the heaven for 7 or 11,
He pays homage to the last when he rolled a two
and six,
Two – for the guilt that he held onto,
All the pleasures disguised in love,
The food, the lust, the drinks, the drugs,
He now creates his reality from a space of love,
Replaced immoral temptations with the glory of
trust,

Transformed like a butterfly caressed in Eden's stardust,
And six – for his lack of sense of the 6th,
He never knew sense of the 6th,
Trying to make sense of the 6th,
He meditates on the 6th,
Now he can see his path through the 6th,
Until now, he was concerned with the not knowing of the knowing,
But he came to realize letting go of knowing is the knowing,
The energy of the universe flowing through him to guide him on this journey he is going,
Before he takes this leap of faith, there's one questions that remains,
Would you rather die on purpose or die off purpose?
He jumps, and he doesn't fall,
He rises in the ecstasy of love, above all,
Some say, you only live once,
I say, you only live now,
And if now is my forever,
I will forever leap from each cliff with no regard to safety or risk,
I will rise in the abyss of my higher calling,
My purpose...

Independence Day

On this day of independence,
I liberate my mind from this life sentence,
Of being what I'm supposed to be,
I am free, from the programming of a matrix
society,
I am me, more than what the eyes can see,
And only what the eye can see,
Labels are for those who are comfortable in
containers,
Arrows are for those who have lost their way,
I am neither,
Standards are for those who need to belong,
Programs are for those who require instruction,
I am neither,
I am that I am, and I cannot be taught the I am from
any source other than I am,
I take off my shoes,
Because I have walked the path of mindlessness for
too long,
It's time to divert from that path to find my own,
I take off my shirt,
Along with all labels society has casted on me,
I am beyond what thought can perceive, and all the
things I was made to believe,
I take off my pants,
This is nothing you'll see in a model magazine or on
TV,
Raw and uncut, no literally raw and uncut,
As children, we should have been taught that our
bodies are uniquely enough,
And I take off my underwear,
There is nothing but beauty under here,
I am now in my natural state of being,

Can you go past body image, judgment, or anything
the ego is seeing?
And be in this body, without perception of the body,
I never knew that nudity could feel so freeing,
It's a shame that I can only feel this freedom at
Gunnison beach,
And as I continue to grow and release,
Be aware, there will be a day when I go nude on the
streets...

High School Lessons

She never left me alone,
Like flesh to a bone,
She wore me out,
She wore me in,
Another detention for different colored Tims,
Dress code infraction,
Constant dissatisfaction,
Became mold to my reaction,
I never knew the higher purpose of her actions,
On my case, she was on my case,
Like bad breath too close to the face,
I couldn't breathe,
I couldn't see,
That she was guiding me,
To be a better me,
The best I'll ever be.

She never left me alone,
The opposite of interactions in his home,
She wanted more, demanded more,
Out of me,
Constantly, correcting me,
It had to be done perfectly,
I knew nothing of the *12 Angry Men* that she taught,
But she fought, for that 1 angry boy that saw,
She knew a potential in me that I was too blind to
see within myself.

She never left me alone,
To prepare me to stand on my own,
Strong, enough to withstand society's impurities,
Breaking through insecurities to see a life of more
than it appeared to be,

She put faith in me,
She was more than just a teacher,
She was the evening sports feature,
At every game cheering in every vein,
She cheered when I scored and cheered when I
didn't,
A love without condition is always winning,
She was more than a teacher,
She was like a Sunday preacher,
And life was her sermon,
I was a member of her congregation learning,
And she was determined, like a firefighter saving
every child in a house that was burning,
She always did more.

Mrs. Burkett taught me the best life lesson,
That you can love beyond profession,
That you can care without question,
And family is without complexion,
I'm happy she never left me alone,
And now that I'm grown,
I'm grateful for her guiding light,
And I hold in my heart all the love and support she
has always shown...

Joey Raines

Before your eyes, you see the beam of light from a
shooting star,
The illumination of light that has been felt from
those near and far,
Be careful not to gaze for too long,
The radiance from his aura will glare too strong,
You gave a false claim to the fame of the dark city,
And to that name we're estranged, this is now the
heart city.

Our rising star,
Your life has proven that you are,
Not one that has lost its way,
But a star that has fallen into place,
And into that place,
You are in infinite space,
We'll forever reminisce of your smile and grace...

Rest in Love, Brother

Grateful Encounters (1)

To the woman who told me that I'm in the wrong profession,
That I should be a Ralph Lauren model,
I'm glad you didn't see me,
I'm happy you didn't see how unappealing my insides are,
The debris from the wreckage,
Feelings of being alone, abused, and neglected,
This life on the surface is what you see,
But what if you could see who I really am, the inside me?
Imagine, we changed our lenses, and modeling was only for your inner being,
The raw beauty of our souls would be on the stage for all to see,
Would you still consider me a model?
Would you still find me attractive enough?
Or would you tell me that modeling school is the best option for me?
Or maybe, just maybe, you'll tell me modeling isn't my thing,
There's just too many marks, too many scars, and you're a little too thin,
After all, this isn't the type of modeling for the malnourished,
You have to feed your soul and put into it what you want out of it,
Yes, this is certainly the plus-sized kind of modeling,
Maybe you would tell me if I want to model, I'll need just a little bit of work,
Maybe not now, but I'll make sure we get there together,

Because the beauty in your soul would refuse to
leave mine alone and cold,
This is the same beauty that spoke words of comfort
to a complete stranger,
The same beauty that walked through miserable
habits of daily routine with a glowing smile,
Maybe, actually most definitely,
I would have stopped, to say that you are gorgeous,
And your amazing grace caresses my soul and cures
the depths of depression,
And you should be a model...

Grateful Encounters (3)

To the man who said,
You are Christian cause you smile,
Thanks for showing me...

Family Ties

Do you think of me,
Did you think of me,
Do you ever wonder about me?
The urge to see me,
I am here,
You are there,
Distance filled with rivers of tears,
Guilt, shame, blame,
Look at me,
Say something,
Tell me that you care,
Tell me that you don't care,
But don't you dare,
Act like this didn't happen!

Tell me something,
Tell me anything,
Tell me the truth,
I can handle the truth,
Tell me if I should've been missing you,
I can handle it,
I am strong,
Strong enough to cry,
Strong enough to move on,
Show me emotion,
Love or hate,
Trust me I can relate,
Blood has been lost,
Hearts have been crossed,
I've accepted the cost.

I'm no longer a little boy,
I no longer wonder where you are,
Or why you weren't here,
But please just tell me the truth,
I've wondered about you,
Hoping we would rejoice in reunion,
Living dreams of delusion,
I found myself,
In the mist of confusion,
Family ties untied,
Putting pride aside,
No need to hide,
From your shameful disguise,
I am now grown,
And the little boy you once knew,
Has given up on caring for you,
And apparently, you have too...

Lean on Me

We hope to escape mortality,
And return to a world of morality,
We hope to escape fatality,
And return to our neighbors of hospitality,
We hope for the better,
Like Dr. King said to walk hand in hand together,
But we grew into a people,
That treat each other less than equal,
We can't even see through those who are supposed
to be true,
Who knew this is what the world would come to?
Pain and despair,
Happiness is rare,
Unaware you're born into world that's unfair,
If you died tomorrow who would truly care?
But keep hope alive,
Because a new day will arrive,
To the best we have to strive,
Cause our dreams help us survive,
We have to live through our hopes and dreams,
Not the daily routine!
We can't look back to where all the time went,
Even though our dreams seem distant,
Our hope keeps us persistent...

Big Brother

They say our mission is too important to fail,
And if done right, with all your might, new life will prevail,
This is more than a match, much more than a friend,
This is a brotherhood that I once dreamed of,
One I was cheated of,
But one I didn't defend,
For now, his life is in its precious stage of infinite,
And when little black boys begin to wonder where their fathers went,
Five years ago, you were a boy with the mind of a sponge,
Emotions unplugged,
A song unsung,
No one can foresee a brotherhood's outcome,
Or what it should strive to become,
But I can no longer compete with my brother's reaper,
No, he is not kin and this is not blood –
It's much, much deeper,
In time, he will know my back to be the bridge as his steps in life become steeper,
Because one thing is for sure, through it all,
I'll eternally be my brother's keeper...

August 29th, 2017

Today
There was no sunrise,
The clouds were dark,
The ocean was rough,
The waves were fierce,
The wind was strong,
The birds were persistent,
The sand was turbulent,
Joggers jogged, walkers walked,
There was no sunrise,
Will there be a sunset?
I smile, with a tear in eye,
Giving gratitude and thankfulness,
For the ability to feel and experience life,
In both love and pain,
The wonder of existence is found,
I am able to see both worlds,
Nature shows me the path,
Today
There was a sunrise,
But it was naked to the human eye,
Clouds were a forecast of yang and yin,
The ocean deliberately stroked the shoreline,
Birds glided through the wind, allowing their wings
to rest with fate,
A group of women pass gossiping on a TV show,
A familiar face,
Pastor Sony joyfully says "Hi" on his daily walk,
There was much movement and life,
There was much beauty inside,
There was a sunrise,
And there will always be a sunset...

I Remember

I Remember...
As a young boy, I wanted to be President,
To lead a revolution of love
Now, as a young soul, I just want to lead a
revolution of love.

I Remember...
My teenage years, eating pizza, a lot of pizza,
Actually, entire pizzas,
I probably shouldn't have eaten all that pizza.

I Remember...
That night seeing you lying on the kitchen floor,
Victim to your own insecurities,
Your selfishness of passing off your impurities,
My selfishness, hoping this will all end,
When will a mother's pain begin to end?

I Remember...
My first heartbreak, and soaking in my guilt,
Because I was the reason for your heart's ache,
I guess that was the script for lover's fate.

I Remember...
When Maria told me to change the world,
To begin with children, cause they are our future,
I hope she knows I kept my word with every ounce
of energy,
From my heart to yours.

I Remember...
That one-night stand,
Your smile was a forecast of sunshine,

As snow flurries sprinkled the sky,
One-night stands are better when we only penetrate
our minds,
Unconscious of time, we give hopeful goodbyes,
To one day converse again.

I Remember...
My first poem, because that was the beginning of
expression from my soul,
From #2 pencils and memo pads to here today, in
front of this microphone,
I will always, always cherish you.

I Remember...
Not believing in the limitations of MS,
New life forms, when you see none left,
To be told that life would be restricted,
But here is where I found abundance within myself.

I Remember...
That Ugandan child who told me he wanted to be an
entrepreneur,
I hope he fulfills his dreams and creates the cure,
For the sad realities of a country that may not allow
him to be an entrepreneur.

I Remember...
Eight years ago, when I casted my first presidential
vote,
It was like my yearning for justice, and equality
finally spoke,
Or maybe, I was just too young and naïve to see,
Because now, I can't tell the difference,
Between being voiceless and being silenced.

I Remember...
The night I don't want to remember,
16-year-old's shouldn't drug and take advantage of
other 16-year-old's,
You were supposed to be my friend,
What happened?

I Remember...
Your love,
When we held each other so close,
We were one, unified body,
My thoughts were yours, your essence of natural
spring pure,
You were my fatality, and you were my cure,
I wanted more.

I Remember...
Working at the hospital, having patience to take
care of patients,
I won't forget your stubbornness, suffering, and
denial,
I couldn't heal your pain, but I would've done
anything to make you smile.

I Remember...
In 8th grade, breaking my arm in that basketball
game from tripping over my own feet,
Clumsy of me,
Ironically, my relationships tell the same story.

I Remember...
The times giving up!

I Remember...
The times rising up!

And I Remember…
All the memories that brought me to the here and
now,
Because destiny was written to have all of us
together here and now,
We can choose the fortune of our own memories,
Starting here and now,
Peace, compassion, unity are neither past nor future
tense,
They are here and now,
Do not regret, do not wait for the next,
The only moment we have is here and now,
Unconditional love is here and now,
And I will remember this precious memory we all
share, here and now...

Rewriting History

If I had to do it all over again,
I would do it again,
I appreciate all the connections and places I've been,
From that to then,
I'd lose all over again,
Understanding I had to lose to win,
I had to seek out to look within,
To find peace within,
The love within,
To rise from sin,
Yang and Yin,
I'd begin again,
To come to end,
To pretend to blend,
To lose a friend,
And befriend again,
I'd love again,
And hurt all over again,
Breaking hearts,
To amend again,
I'd regret the past,
And forgive again,
I'd speak life into these words again,
Book and pen,
To write these poems again,
I'd bleed emotions again,
And again, all over again,
Finding Zen,
To resend Godsend,
Perishing in your last words,
Falling down again,
To rise and ascend again,
Transcend again,

The light within,
I love you, again,
I'm sorry, again,
Each day, I'm born again,
Each day, I'll die again,
And each day I'd do it again...

The Beginning

If this is the end,
If this is my end,
Then please, strip me of sin,
Let my soul cleanse of all the evils I've been,
Turn my ego, into one for the people,
One for a sequel, that will plague mankind with
deepest dimensions of love and affection,
Let your thoughts of my life be of joyful reflection,
Any hurt I've inflicted be a memory of the past,
Bottled with all the pain in mass to disappear with
my ash,
Let your tears rain throughout for the last,
Let thunder sound as happiness and sadness clash,
Let excitement strike with a lightning flash,
Most importantly, this storm will pass,
And tomorrow's hope is a clear forecast,
To live in memory of me is to live presently,
Acceptance of the past,
No anticipation of the future,
Beloved, you hold the key of eternity within your
presence,
Giving gratitude for all your blessings,
This is the staircase to the heavens...

About the Author

Mychal Mills was born and raised in Neptune Township, New Jersey. He graduated from Monmouth University with a Bachelor of Science in Business Management and an MBA from Monmouth University.

Mychal Co-founded Konscious Youth Development & Service (KYDS) in 2014, a youth development program that focuses on holistic intervention of the body, mind and soul. The organization reflects his personal journey of finding inner peace and balance. He believes any growth is more sustainable through the internal development building tools of love and compassion from within that are transferable in any life situation.

Mychal loves poetry as a creative expression. He's been writing poetry since he was a child. It's been a discovery of emotions and insights. Much of the words in this book were born from introspection, looking deep within. The words of his poems reflect his soul and journey in life.

Final Note

I would like to personally thank you for taking this opportunity to look within yourself. To discover the deepest parts of your being that often go unnoticed. Moving your presence downstream, going with the flow of the current. Allowing your vulnerabilities to rise to surface. Holding your insecurities tight. They become the security and strength to your authentic self.

I believe everything happens for a reason. Relationships, triumphs, and tragedies all happen on purpose. All of my life experiences led to right now. My poems are a reflection of the journey. I look at the synchronicity of events and I'm happy it all unfolded the way it did. Whatever the case, life reveals itself on purpose. And every experience was manifested in my life through my own vibrational frequency. I've had the freedom to react or respond, consciously or unconsciously, to these experiences. This is the beauty of choice.

Some may see the circumstance as life falling apart. I view it as life falling into place.

This book is my reflection through words, emotions, pictures, thoughts, and feelings. Although I love each poem, the truth of my being is in-between the words. Nothing is absolute. Nothing is concrete. Sometimes, I look back on some of the poems with a different awareness and meaning. I think that's why art is so intriguing, the ability to have multiple perspectives over periods of time.

I hope you enjoyed the Experience!

Bless your Heart. Bless your Light.

Peace, Love & Presence,

Mychal